Fun Holiday Crafts
Kids Can Do!

Valentine's Day Crafts

Arlene and
Herbert Erlbach

E **Enslow Publishers, Inc.**

40 Industrial Road   PO Box 38
Box 398   Aldershot
Berkeley Heights, NJ 07922 Hants GU12 6BP
USA   UK

http://www.enslow.com

Dedication
To Cely Weinstein, a person with a big heart.

Copyright © 2004 by Enslow Publishers, Inc.

Library of Congress Cataloging-in-Publication Data

Erlbach, Arlene.
    Valentine's day crafts / Arlene and Herbert Erlbach.
      p. cm. — (Fun holiday crafts kids can do)
    Summary: Provides information about the origin and customs of St. Valentine's Day, ideas for
celebrating this holiday, and directions for making such crafts as a bag of Valentine wishes, a friend-
ship necklace, a lacy Valentine bookmark, and a love bug card.
    Includes bibliographical references and index.
    ISBN 0-7660-2237-4 (hardcover)
    1. Valentine decorations—Juvenile literature. 2. Handicraft—Juvenile literature. [1. Valentine's
Day. 2. Handicraft. 3. Holidays.] I. Erlbach, Herb. II. Title. III. Series.
TT900.V34E75   2004
745.594'1618—dc21

                         2003010331

Printed in the United States of America

10 9 8 7 6 5 4 3 2 1

To Our Readers:
We have done our best to make sure all Internet addresses in this book were active and appropriate
when we went to press. However, the author and the publisher have no control over and assume
no liability for the material available on those Internet sites or on other Web sites they may link to.
Any comments or suggestions can be sent by e-mail to comments@enslow.com or to the address
on the back cover.

Illustration Credits: Crafts prepared by June Ponte.
Photography by Carl Feryok.

Cover Illustration: Carl Feryok

Contents

*Safety Note: Be sure to ask for help from an adult, if needed, to complete these crafts!

Introduction

Each year we celebrate Valentine's Day on February 14. We send and receive heart-shaped cards. We eat red or pink candies and cookies. We tell our friends and family how much we care about them.

No one is sure exactly how Valentine's Day began. It may have started 2,000 years ago. On a Roman holiday called Lupercalia, girls wrote their names on sheets of paper. They put them in a jug. A boy would pick a girl's name out of the jug. The two would become partners for the holiday. Sometimes, the couple would get engaged at the end of the celebration.

There is another story about a cruel Roman emperor who lived in the year 269. He did not want young men to marry. He wanted them for his army instead. A priest named Valentine secretly

Be My Valentine

married the young couples. The emperor found out. On February 14, he had the priest killed.

A different story about Valentine's Day is about another priest who was also named Valentine. He was sent to prison because he refused to pray to the Roman gods. Valentine became friendly with a prison guard. The guard's blind daughter and Valentine fell in love.

Before the emperor had him killed, Valentine wrote the girl a letter. When she opened it, a miracle happened. She could see. The letter was signed "from your Valentine."

Bag of Valentine Wishes

Make a collection of Valentine wishes. Put them in a pretty bag to give as a present.

What You Will Need:

- small paper bag (about 4 by 6 inches)
- markers, glitter pens, crayons, or stickers
- construction paper
- scissors
- craft sticks
- white glue
- red or white tissue paper

1. Decorate the paper bag with markers, glitter pens, crayons, or stickers.

2. Fold the sheet of red construction paper into rectangles.

3. Cut out the rectangles. Then, cut them into hearts. If you like, use the patterns on page 26.

4. Write messages on the back of the craft sticks.

5. Glue the paper hearts to the front of the craft sticks. Decorate the front of the sticks.

6. Place the tissue paper in your bag so that the Valentine sticks can stand up. Arrange the Valentine sticks in the bag.

Start by decorating a bag. . .

Fold and cut your paper. Then, cut out hearts. . .

PICK ME

U·R·COOL

BE MINE

Add colorful messages. . .

Share your great-looking bag with others!

Holiday Hint:

Use the bag as a centerpiece for a Valentine's Day party. Or, give it to a special friend or relative as a holiday present.

BE MINE

Friendship Necklace

This necklace is made by pasting materials made of paper to a surface. Then, they are sealed to make them permanent. This art form is called decoupage.

What You Will Need:

- poster board
- pencil
- scissors
- hole punch
- paper materials (gift wrap, construction paper, etc.)
- white glue
- small bowl or paper cup
- water
- paintbrush
- wax paper
- yarn

1. Draw a heart shape on the poster board. If you like, use the pattern on page 26. Cut the heart out.

2. Glue on scraps of paper materials to decorate your heart. Let them dry on a sheet of wax paper.

3. In the small bowl or paper cup, mix up a thin glue "soup." Use three parts glue to one part water. Brush the glue mixture over the heart and let it dry overnight on the wax paper.

4. Cut your heart in half, puzzle style. Punch a hole at the top of each curve of the heart, as shown. Then, tie a piece of yarn through the hole in each half of the heart.

Cut out a heart and
add colorful paper. . .

Make a puzzle-
shaped cut. . .

Share your finished
necklace with a friend!

Holiday Hint:

Give one half of the necklace
to a special friend. Keep the
other half to remind you of
how important you are to
each other.

BE
MINE

Fold-Up Valentine Surprise

Inside this Valentine there is a message and a surprise gift!

What You Will Need:

- red construction paper
- pencil
- scissors
- white glue
- doily
- stickers
- small toy or candy
- clear tape

1. Fold both sheets of paper in half. Draw half a heart (use the pattern on page 26, if you like) on the fold of one of the pieces. Holding both sheets together, cut out the heart. This will give you two hearts of the same size.

2. Glue the hearts so that the bottom point of one heart is attached to the center of the other heart. Let the glue dry.

3. Write a message on the doily. Then, glue the doily to the center of the heart.

4. Decorate the hearts with stickers or paint markers. Tape a small toy or candy to the middle of the doily.

5. Fold the hearts to the center, as shown. Close the Valentine with clear tape.

Start by gluing the bottoms of your hearts together. . .

Add a Valentine's Day message to your heart. . .

Be My Valentine

Be My Valentine

Decorate the card. . .

Holiday Hint:

Tape it shut and give your beautiful card to someone special!

Give this Valentine to someone who means a lot to you. The person will know you think he or she is special.

BE MINE

Amore Napkin Rings

Amore is Italian for "love." Set a pretty Valentine's Day table with these festive napkin rings.

What You Will Need:

- empty toilet paper roll
- ruler
- pencil
- scissors
- red felt and felt in a contrasting color
- white glue

1. Mark off four 1-inch sections on the toilet paper roll. Squeeze the roll flat to cut the pieces.
2. Carefully, cut the red felt into strips large enough to cover each napkin ring.
3. Glue a strip of red felt to each piece.
4. Cut heart shapes out of the contrasting color of felt.
5. Glue the hearts onto the napkin ring pieces. Let them dry.

Start by cutting out the rings. . .

Use red felt to cover the rings. . .

Finish your ring by adding some hearts. . .

Holiday Hint:

Your napkin ring adds a festive touch to any Valentine's Day meal!

Use your napkin rings for a Valentine's Day party or give them as a gift.

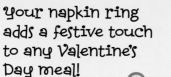
BE MINE

Valentine Cat

This Valentine cat has a tail with a message.

What You Will Need:

- red construction paper
- fine-tip marker or pen
- scissors
- white glue
- wiggle eyes
- yarn
- felt (optional)
- glitter (optional)

1. Fold the red construction paper in half to form two rectangles. Draw half a heart (use the pattern on p. 26, if you like) and cut it out. This will be the cat's body.

2. Repeat Step 1, making a smaller heart for the cat's head.

3. Position the hearts as shown and glue the pointed ends together. The top heart can overlap the bottom heart.

4. Cut two triangles from the red paper scraps for the cat's ears, or use the patterns on p. 28. Glue them on and let them dry.

5. Cut a strip of curved paper for the cat's tail, as shown. Glue it to the cat's back and let it dry.

6. Glue on the wiggle eyes. Let them dry. Then, draw a nose and some stripes with the marker or pen.

7. Glue on some yarn for whiskers. If you like, add some felt for a soft belly and some glitter for the ears.

Start by folding the paper
and cutting out a heart . . .

Glue the hearts
together. . .

Make some ears. . .

Your cat is ready
to celebrate!

Holiday Hint:

Write a message on the
cat's tail. Then, give this
Valentine greeting to
someone special!

BE
MINE

BE
MINE

Lacy Valentine Bookmark

Save a place in your favorite book with this bookmark made with lacy Valentine hearts.

What You Will Need:

- red construction paper
- pencil
- scissors
- white glue
- 3- by 6-inch piece of oak tag or lightweight cardboard

- crayons or markers
- hole punch
- yarn or ribbon

1. Draw different heart shapes on the red construction paper. If you like, use the patterns on page 26. Cut out the hearts.

2. Glue the hearts to the oak tag or cardboard. Decorate the bookmark with crayons or markers.

3. Punch a hole in the top of the bookmark.

4. Thread the pieces of yarn or ribbon through the hole. Tie a knot about 1 inch from the end to form a tassel.

Cut out some hearts to decorate
your bookmark. . .

Add some yarn
or ribbon. . .

Use the markers
for the finishing
touches!

Holiday Hint:

Lacy bookmarks are nice
presents to give to your
favorite bookworm on
Valentine's Day.

BE
MINE

17

Love Bug Card

This love bug hides special messages under its wings. It shows someone how much you care!

What You Will Need:

- ½ sheet red construction paper
- scissors
- ¼ sheet black construction paper
- pen or fine-tip marker
- construction paper in contrasting colors

- wiggle eyes
- white glue
- glitter (optional)
- black pipe cleaner
- clear tape

1. Fold the corners of the red construction paper as shown to make flaps. These will be the bug's wings.

2. Cut a heart shape from the black paper to form the bug's head.

3. Write Valentine messages beneath each wing.

4. Cut hearts out of the contrasting colors of paper to decorate the bug's wings.

5. Glue on the hearts and wiggle eyes. Let the glue dry. If you like, add some glitter to make the bug sparkle.

6. Cut the pipe cleaner in half. Tape the two pieces onto the head for antennae.

Write a special
Valentine's Day
message. . .

I only have
eyes for you!

Cut out hearts and add
them to the wings. . .

Start by folding the
paper into wings. . .

Add the eyes and
antennae. . .

Holiday Hint:

Your love bug
is finished!

Give your love bug card
to someone you love!

BE
MINE

19

Heart Ornament

This is a pretty ornament to hang up on Valentine's Day.

What You Will Need:

- red or pink construction paper
- scissors
- glitter pens, sequins, or stickers
- hole punch
- ribbon or yarn
- white glue

1. Fold a sheet of paper in half lengthwise.

2. Fold it in half again. Keep folding the paper lengthwise until you have eight sections.

3. Cut your folded paper into heart shapes. Then, open up the paper and cut it into a large heart, as shown.

4. Decorate the heart with glitter pens, sequins, or stickers.

5. Punch holes in the top of each section, as shown. Loop the ribbon or yarn through the holes and glue the ends to the back. Tape up your ornament.

Start by folding
your paper. . .

Cut heart shapes out
of the paper. . .

Cut the folded paper into
a heart and add some
ribbon and flowers!

Holiday Hint:

Hang your ornament
where it will remind you
of Valentine's Day!

BE
MINE

Valentine Butterfly Paper Clip

This butterfly can be a giant paper clip to give as a Valentine's Day present.

What You Will Need:

- tissue paper
- spring-style clothespin
- construction paper
- scissors

- white glue
- wiggle eyes
- markers or glitter
- black pipe cleaner

1. Fold the tissue paper in half. Fold it half again.

2. Pinch the center of the paper. Insert it into the clothespin.

3. Cut the construction paper into a heart for the butterfly's head. Glue it to the top of the closed end of the clothespin. Let it dry.

4. Glue on the wiggle eyes. Let the glue dry.

5. Use the markers or glitter to make tiny hearts on the butterfly's body.

6. Cut the pipe cleaner in half. Fold the pieces to make antennae. Put a dab of glue in the center of the antennae. Insert them into the clothespin. Let them dry.

Start by folding the tissue paper into a butterfly shape...

Cut a heart for the butterfly's head...

Add a face and antennae and your butterfly is finished!

Holiday Hint:

Add a strip of magnetic tape to the butterfly to make a festive refrigerator magnet.

BE MINE

Sun Catcher Heart

Hang this sun catcher in the window to see the sun come through.

What You Will Need:

- white paper plate
- scissors
- red or pink tissue paper
- wax paper
- white tissue paper
- white glue
- water
- small bowl or paper cup
- paintbrush
- hole punch
- ribbon or yarn
- doily (optional)

1. Carefully cut out the center of the paper plate. Then, cut hearts from the red or pink tissue paper.

2. Place the plate on the wax paper face down. Place the white tissue paper over the plate so that the opening is covered.

3. Mix up a thin glue "soup" in the small bowl or paper cup. Use three parts glue to one part water. Stir with the paintbrush, and brush the tissue paper with the glue mixture.

4. Turn the plate over. Glue one heart to the center of the tissue paper. Glue the other hearts to the plate.

5. Leave the plate on the wax paper. Let it dry overnight.

6. When the plate is dry, carefully pull off the wax paper. Punch a hole in the top. Loop the ribbon or yarn through. If you like, you can punch extra holes and loop the ribbon or yarn all the way around, and add a doily for a lacy edge.

Cut out the center of the paper plate. . .

Mix the water and glue. . .

Cut some tissue paper. . .

Add the ribbon and doily for a nice finish. . .

Hang your beautiful sun catcher in a window!

Holiday Hint:

Hang this pretty sun catcher in your window or give it as a gift to someone you love.

BE MINE

25

Patterns

Use tracing paper to copy the patterns on these pages. Ask an adult to help you cut and trace the shapes onto construction paper.

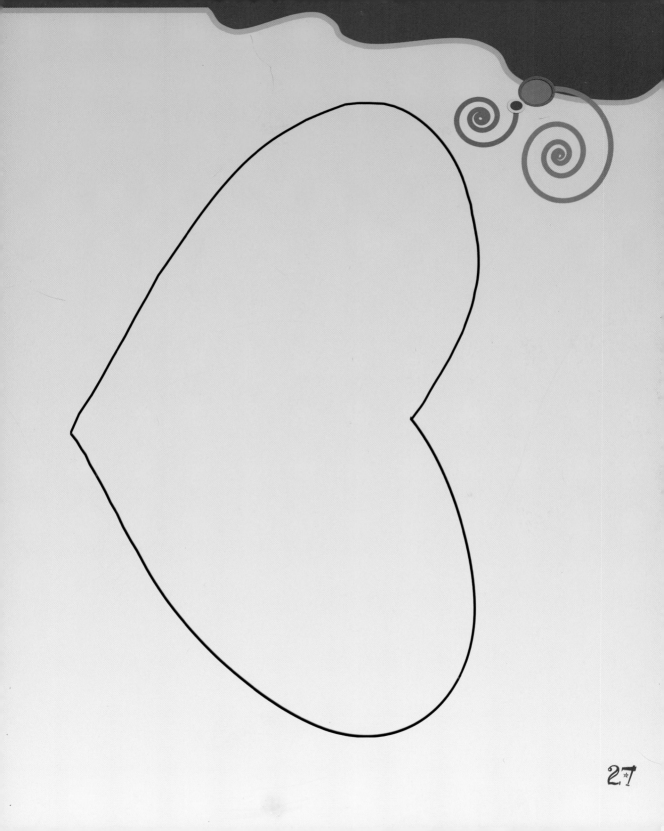

27

Reading About Valentine's Day

Brownrigg, Sheri. *Hearts & Crafts.* Berkeley, Calif.: Tricycle Press, 1996.

Bulla, Clyde Robert. *The Story of Valentine's Day.* New York: HarperCollins Publishers, 1999.

Graham-Barber, Lynda. *Mushy!: The Complete Book of Valentine Words.* New York: Bradbury Press, 1991.

Landau, Elaine. *Valentine's Day—Candy, Love, and Hearts.* Berkeley Heights, N.J.: Enslow Publishers, 2001.

Roop, Peter, and Connie Roop. *Let's Celebrate Valentine's Day.* Brookfield, Conn.: Millbrook Press, 1999.

Ross, Kathy. *All New Crafts for Valentine's Day.* Brookfield, Conn.: Millbrook Press, 2002.

Internet Addresses

PBS Kids: Happy Valentine's Day

Check out this site for Valentine's Day games, coloring pages, and e-cards.

<http://pbskids.org/vday.html>

The History Channel: Valentine's Day

This fun Web site contains information on the origins of Valentine's Day and more!

<http://historychannel.com/exhibits/valentine>

index